A Facing History and Ourselves Publication

IDENTITY AND BELONGING IN A CHANGING GREAT BRITAIN

FACING
HISTORY
AND
OURSELVES

Facing History and Ourselves is an international educational and professional development organization whose mission is to engage students of diverse backgrounds in an examination of racism, prejudice, and antisemitism in order to promote the development of a more humane and informed citizenry. By studying the historical development of the Holocaust and other examples of genocide, students make the essential connection between history and the moral choices they confront in their own lives. For more information about Facing History and Ourselves, please visit our website at *www.facinghistory.org*.

Facing History and Ourselves⬧ is a trademark registered in the U.S. Patent & Trademark Office.

Cover art photo: Cover photograph by Charlie Colmer

To order classroom copies, please fax a purchase order to 617-232-0281 or call 617-232-1595 to place a phone order.

To receive additional copies of this resource, please visit *www.facinghistory.org/identityandbelonging*.

ISBN-13: 978-0-9798440-9-6

Facing History and Ourselves Ltd.
375 Kensingston High St.
London W14 8QH
United Kingdom
(011) 44 207 471 5540
www.facinghistory.com

FACING
HISTORY
AND
OURSELVES

ABOUT FACING HISTORY AND OURSELVES

Facing History and Ourselves is a non-profit educational organization whose mission is to engage students of diverse backgrounds in an examination of racism, prejudice, and antisemitism, in order to promote a more humane and informed citizenry. As the name Facing History and Ourselves implies, the organization helps teachers and their students make the essential connections between history and the moral choices they confront in their own lives, and offers a framework and a vocabulary for analysing the meaning and responsibility of citizenship and the tools to recognize bigotry and indifference in their own worlds. Through a rigourous examination of the failure of democracy in Germany during the 1920s and 1930s, and the steps leading to the Holocaust, along with other examples of hatred, collective violence, and genocide in the past century, Facing History and Ourselves provides educators with tools for teaching history and ethics, and for helping their students learn to combat prejudice with compassion, indifference with participation, myth and misinformation with knowledge.

Believing that no classroom exists in isolation, Facing History and Ourselves offers programmes and materials to a broad audience of students, parents, teachers, civic leaders, and all of those who play a role in the education of young people. Through significant higher education partnerships, Facing History and Ourselves also reaches and impacts teachers before they enter their classrooms.

By studying the choices that led to critical episodes in history, students learn how issues of identity and membership, ethics, and judgment have meaning today and in the future. Facing History and Ourselves' resource books provide a meticulously researched yet flexible structure for examining complex events and ideas. Educators can select appropriate readings and draw upon additional resources available online, or from our comprehensive lending library.

Our foundational resource book, *Facing History and Ourselves: Holocaust and Human Behavior*, embodies a sequence of study that begins with identity—first individual identity, and then group and national identities, with their definitions of membership. From there, the programme examines the failure of democracy in Germany and the steps leading to the Holocaust—the most documented case of twentieth-century indifference, dehumanization, hatred, racism, antisemitism, and mass murder. It goes on to explore difficult questions of judgement, memory, and legacy, and the necessity for responsible participation to prevent injustice. Facing History and Ourselves then returns to the theme of civic participation to examine stories of individuals, groups, and nations who have worked to build just and inclusive communities and whose stories illuminate the courage, compassion, and political will that are needed to protect democracy today and in generations to come. Other examples in which civic dilemmas test democracy, such as the Armenian Genocide and the U.S. civil rights movement, expand and deepen the connection between history and the choices we face today and in the future.

Facing History and Ourselves has offices or resource centers in the United States, Canada, and the United Kingdom as well as in-depth partnerships in Rwanda, South Africa, and Northern Ireland. Facing History and Ourselves' outreach is global, with educators trained in more than 80 countries, and delivery of our resources through a website accessed worldwide with online content delivery, a programme for international fellows, and a set of NGO partnerships. By convening conferences of scholars, theologians, educators, and journalists, Facing History and Ourselves' materials are kept timely, relevant, and responsive to salient issues of global citizenship in the twenty-first century.

For more than 30 years, Facing History and Ourselves has challenged students and educators to connect the complexities of the past to the moral and ethical issues of today. They explore democratic values, and consider what it means to exercise one's rights and responsibilities in the service of a more humane and compassionate world. They become aware that 'little things are big'—seemingly minor decisions can have a major impact and change the course of history.

For more about Facing History and Ourselves, visit our website at *www.facinghistory.org*.

ACKNOWLEDGEMENTS

Primary Writer and Editor: Adam Strom

Facing History and Ourselves greatly appreciates Deutsche Bank for its support to produce *Identity and Belonging in a Changing Great Britain*—a resource developed to give UK educators a tool to discuss social, religious and cultural difference in the classroom. Creating this project has been a wonderfully collaborative experience at Facing History and Ourselves. There are so many people to thank for their good work on this project: Karen Murphy and Carrie Supple worked together on the first drafts of this resource. Adam Strom wrote and edited the final version of this book. Jennifer Gray provided invaluable research support, and found many of the photographs that illustrate the text; we will miss her contributions. Mangala Nanda joined the project team and offered important editorial guidance, and for this we cannot thank her enough. Maria Hill, Stephanie Hawkins, and Catherine O'Keefe made certain the thinking behind this project was ultimately captured on the page and turned into a book. Sharon Lindenburger kept us grammatically in line by copy-editing the manuscript, while The Herman Lewis Design Syndicate creatively brought the pages to life with its sophisticated cover and page design. Special thanks to Rachel Murray who oversaw and developed the resource's web presence. Michael McIntyre, Facing History and Ourselves, UK Programme Coordinator in London, provided important context and conversation on issues of British identity. Margot Stern Strom, Marty Sleeper, and Marc Skvirsky were a thoughtful and supportive editorial team. We sincerely thank Seth Klarman for his critical feedback during the draft stage. We also want to thank Judy Wise who understood the importance of these resources for our teachers, and Larisa Pazimo who served as our liaison to Deutsche Bank.

Sponsored by

Facing History and Ourselves depends on the wisdom of teachers for insight into the practical uses of all its resources in the classroom. Many teachers piloted *Identity and Belonging in a Changing Great Britain* in its early stage so that future classrooms could benefit. For this we acknowledge: Jo Upton, Una Sookin, Mari Williams, Matt Williams, Carrie McCarty, Vanessa Hull, and Ruth-Anne Lenga (Consultant).

Table of Contents

PREFACE

As this book goes to press, the global economy has entered what many economists and historians are calling the worst recession since the 1930s. People are looking for security. Who will protect them? Who is to blame? Scholars warn us that in hard times many look for scapegoats. National groups once considered on the fringe have exploited this anxiety to recruit new members. Their poll numbers have risen throughout Europe.

Those who are following the heated debates about immigration, culture, and British identity might get the impression that until recently Great Britain's identity has been unchanged for centuries. In fact, Great Britain's identity has never been static and a quick survey of British history reveals that migration, far from being the exception, has been part of almost every era. This resource will help teachers and students gain perspective as they participate in the national civic dialogue.

Before the formal establishment of the British Empire, the Island was invaded by Romans, Vikings, Saxons, and Normans. Later, merchants from the Netherlands and other European kingdoms made their way to Britain. As early as the 1600s, Asians and later Africans were living in Britain, first in smaller numbers, and soon in larger numbers as slaves. After the establishment of the United Kingdom, Irish settlers came to England, first for opportunity, and later to escape the potato famine. Indian and Chinese traders settled in port cities and helped the Empire prosper. Huguenot refugees settled in the East End area of London only to be replaced by Eastern European Jews. More recently, Bengalis have moved into the same streets. Each of these groups, in large and small ways, changed the meaning of being British.

After World War II and the decline of the Empire, immigration has been increasingly visible. Some use the arrival of the Windrush, a boat with nearly 500 Jamaicans who were recruited from the Caribbean to

West Indian Immigrants at Victoria Station, London 1956

help rebuild Great Britain after the Blitz, to symbolize the arrival of migrant workers to the British Isles. They were followed by thousands of Asians from the former British colony of India, seeking economic opportunities. In the 1970s and 1980s, migrants from East Africa and Uganda made Great Britain their home. Despite these waves of immigration, Great Britain is not 'over-run' with immigrants; migrants make up about 10 per cent of the British population. However, there is great diversity within this 10 per cent. One can hear approximately 250 different languages spoken on the streets of London. And, at the same time, second and third generation migrants often struggle with their parents' and grandparents' native tongues.

Globalization has hastened migration. Immigration accounted for nearly half of Great Britain's population growth between 1991 and 2001. Today, the children and grandchildren of immigrants go to school and work beside the children and grandchildren of families who can trace their family's history to the British Isles for centuries.

British immigrants protest new proposed immigration restrictions.

It was not only globalization that brought people here; the technologies of our era make communication across oceans possible in ways that previous generations could never have imagined. Shops sell pre-paid phone cards offering inexpensive rates to ring up families 'back home.' It is not only the phone that connects people to their traditional homelands; it is also current technology. Through the internet and satellite television, migrants watch television, download movies, participate in virtual communities, and even read the daily news from their old homelands and in their new one.

Some see the increased diversity in Great Britain and worry that it somehow eats away at the core of British identity. Again, the historical picture is more complicated than one might imagine. Despite facing prejudice, Jewish and Catholic communities have long established roots in Great Britain. The stories of religious minorities in the past have much to offer both newcomers and historically British families. Even though the Church of England is the established church of the land, it too is negotiating its role in a largely secular society. In fact, newcomers from former West Indian colonies have helped re-populate a number of churches experiencing declining attendance.

Many of these issues surrounding British identity and Britishness have been in the background for years. These issues were heightened by recent developments within the European Union, which demanded reflection on both the country's European heritage as well as its distinct British character. Tour guides at the Tower of London routinely play on such connections when they ask 'Who is here from Great Britain?' followed up by 'Who is here from Europe?' When the British drop their hands, guides ask, 'Are we not European as well?'

Yet it was the terrorist attacks on 7 July 2005 that brought the discussion of British identity to the fore. Why would young men, raised in Great Britain, have committed such a brutal attack on their own citizens? What is their education? Their religion? Their nationality? Was this a failure of integration and multiculturalism? In the aftermath of the attacks, questions about intergration filled the media. Are there equal obligations on the long ensconced and the newly arrived to compromise their core values? What is the obligation of newcomers to fit in? Some critics wondered that if people were not intending to make the attempt to fit in, why did they come?

Since the end of the twentieth century, the convergence of migration and globalization has reshaped the public debate about differences. These already difficult dialogues have been complicated by terrorism and a resurgence of ethnic violence. Whereas once a single language, a single skin color, or a shared faith was seen as defining a community, the time has come for a new definition that acknowledges differences, and finds common meaning and purpose in ideals and hopes that transcend history and genealogy. As new ideas, customs, and people make their way into older, more traditional communities, immigration raises dilemmas for migrants and non-migrants alike. For as new arrivals reshape the landscapes of public spaces, they also change our perceptions of home and self.

How can the world's teachers help students deal with the new, the unfamiliar, and the complex? How will students learn to see the perspective of another in order to understand whether the newly arrived and the long ensconced have to compromise their core values? What can educators do to promote tolerance, respect, and understanding?

By focusing on individuals and groups, newcomers and natives alike, the stories in this book raise important questions to provoke reflection and learning regarding the themes of identity, citizenship, and belonging. Used in excerpts or as a whole, these readings will enhance a number of subjects across the curriculum including citizenship, religion, and history.

This resource adds new layers to Facing History and Ourselves' scope and sequence of educational resources. All of our seminars and workshops begin by exploring the relationship between the individual and society. This resource is the first to explore these ideas in a British context. However, it would be a mistake to teach this story in isolation. Facing History and Ourselves resources, such as *Facing History and Ourselves: Holocaust and Human Behavior; Race and Membership in American History; Becoming American: The Chinese Experience; Stories of Identity: Religion, Migration and Belonging in a Changing World;* and *What Do We Do with a Difference?: France and the Debate over Headscarves in Schools,* explore many of these issues within different historical and national contexts. Facing History and Ourselves' 32 years of experience in classrooms around the world have taught us that often the distance one has from the immediate history and reality of a nation can provide an opportunity to reflect on how similar issues are having an impact in our daily lives and allow us to re-imagine solutions to what can seem like entrenched differences and unsolveable conflicts. To purchase or download a copy of any of the aforementioned resources, please visit *www.facinghistory.org/publications.* Links to relevant resources can also be found on our website in the Facing Today section. For a direct link, visit *www.facinghistory.org/facingtoday.*

IMMIGRATION AND IDENTITY

In our globalized world, each of us finds ourselves—in big and small ways—living with differences. Migration and immigration are the most visible examples. Today nearly 200 million people and their children are living in countries outside of their birthplaces. That experience has an impact upon the identities of immigrants and non-immigrants alike. Cultural psychologist Carola Suárez-Orozco writes that for children of immigrants, 'the task of immigration…is creating a transcultural identity.' She explains, 'These youth must creatively fuse aspects of two or more cultures—the parental tradition and the new culture or cultures. In so doing, they synthesize an identity that does not require them to choose between cultures but incorporates traits of both cultures.'[1]

The immigrants and the children of immigrants create new identities by blending traditions from their ancestral homelands and their new homes.

Poet Sujata Bhatt, an emigrant from India, expresses the challenges of fusing her identities in the poem 'The Search for My Tongue.'

You ask me what I mean
by saying I have lost my tongue.
I ask you, what would you do
if you had two tongues in your mouth,
and lost the first one, the mother tongue,
and could not really know the other,
the foreign tongue.

You could not use them both together
even if you thought that way.

And if you lived in a place you had to
speak a foreign tongue,
your mother tongue would rot,
rot and die in your mouth
until you had to spit it out.

I thought I spit it out
but overnight while I dream,

મને હતું કે આખ્ખી જીભ આખ્ખી ભાષા,

(munay hutoo kay aakheejeebh aakhee bhasha)

મેં થૂંકી નાખી છે.

(may thoonky nakhi chay)

પરં તુ રાત્રે સ્વપ્નામાં મારી ભાષા પાછી આવે છે.

(parantoo rattray svupnama man bhasha pachi aavay chay)

ફૂલની જેમ મારી ભાષા મારી જીભ

(foolnee jaim man bhasha man jeebh)

મોઢામાં ખીલે છે.

(modhama kheelay chay)

ફૂલની જેમ મારી ભાષા મારી જીભ

(fullnee jaim man bhasha man jeebh)

મોઢામાં પાકે છે.

(modhama pakay chay)

it grows back, a stump of a shoot
grows longer, grows moist, grows strong veins,
it ties the other tongue in knots,
the bud opens, the bud opens in my mouth,
it pushes the other tongue aside.

Every time I think I've forgotten,
I think I've lost the mother tongue,
it blossoms out of my mouth.[2]

CONNECTIONS

1. Suárez-Orozco says that the task of immigration is to fuse a transcultural identity. What does she mean?

2. In the poem, 'The Search for my Tongue', Bhatt uses the image of two tongues as a way to think about her multiple identities. In the poem, there i s a conflict between the two tongues. To what extent is that struggle natural or inevitable? Is it a difficulty or can it be a source of strength?

3. Carola Suárez-Orozco believes that transcultural identities give immigrant youth an advantage in a globalized world because they can maintain 'two tongues.' What do you think she means? What advantages might she be talking about?

4. According to Carola Suárez-Orozco:

   > For the children of immigrants the task is to braid together[,] into a flexible sense of self, elements of the parent culture, the new culture they are navigating along with an emerging globalized youth culture. For those in the host society, the challenge is to broaden the cultural horizon to incorporate the changing perspectives, habits, and potentials of its diverse newcomers.[3]

   Have you encountered these challenges in your own life? How have you seen instances where they have been successfully overcome?

---

[1] Carola Suárez-Orozco, 'Formulating Identity in a Globalized World', *Globalization: Culture and Education in the New Millennium*, ed. Marcelo Suárez-Orozco and Qin-Hilliard (Berkeley: University of California Press, 2004), 192.

[2] Sujata Bhatt, 'The Search for My Tongue', *Brunizem* (Manchester: Carcanet Press, 1988).

[3] Carola Suárez-Orozco quoted in *Stories of Identity: Religion, Migration, and Belonging in a Changing World* (Brookline: Facing History and Ourselves Foundation, 2008), 117.

An Island of Immigrants

The identities which immigrants forge are shaped by the countries they call home. In *Roots of the Future: Ethnic Diversity in the Making of Britain*, Mayerlene Frow explains that:

> A sense of belonging grows out of the recognition, by individuals and society as a whole, that people from Britain's ethnic minorities are equally citizens, and equally part of British culture...It depends, too, on the ease and the confidence they have that they can fulfill their potential just as easy as anyone else.[1]

Mayerlene Frow asserts that, 'everyone who lives in Britain is either an immigrant or a descendent of an immigrant.' She explains:

> Ethnic diversity is nothing new in Britain. People with different histories, cultures, beliefs and languages have been coming here ever since the beginning of recorded time. Logically, therefore, everyone who lives in Britain is either an immigrant or a descendant of an immigrant. Most of us can probably trace the immigrants in our own personal histories if we go back far enough.
>
> People have come to Britain for many different reasons: some came peacefully as settlers, others were hostile invaders. Thousands arrived as refugees from wars, famines, or civil and religous persecution in their own countries. Some were invited by the monarch or the government to settle here because they had particular skills that were in short supply in Britain. Some were brought here against their will, as slaves or as servants. Throughout the ages, Britain has been a magnet for those seeking a better life, in much the same way as Britons have emigrated, in large numbers, to other parts of the world. International movement has always been a normal part of life...[2]

It is true that Great Britain's demography has never been completely static, and that the movement of people to and from Great Britain has constantly shaped the identity of those who live on this small island. There were Celts and Picts, Angles and Saxons, Romans, and Vikings who settled in Britain. In 1066, the Norman conquest brought further changes to those who lived in the British Isles—changes ranging from legal practices to language. There was even some movement from Africa to Britain in medieval times. These immigrants were generally entertainers linked to royal entourages. However, with the conquest of the New World in the 1500s, and Britain's involvement in the slave trade, people of African origin began appearing as slaves in wealthy English households. This practice was formally stopped only in 1833 when Parliament finally banned all slavery across the British Empire.

While immigration is nothing new, the period after World War II was different, with particularly large-scale non-white immigration to Great Britain. After the war, there was a huge labour shortage throughout the nation, and so the British government began looking for immigrants from its Empire to fill the work force. The government placed advertisements in many countries, encouraging people to come to Great Britain to work. In response to this, large numbers of people from the Caribbean and South Asia moved to Great Britain to fill the labour

Many migrants to England have come from parts of the former empire.

shortage. The 1950s and 1960s were a period of mass immigration to Great Britain. In recent years, the movement of people has continued. Many people have come to Great Britain to flee political persecution, and there has been a growth in applications from asylum seekers.

Cultural psychologist Carola Suárez-Orozco writes:

> Increasing globalization has stimulated an unprecedented flow of immigrants worldwide. These newcomers—from many national origins and a wide range of cultural, religious, linguistic, racial, and ethnic backgrounds—challenge a nation's sense of unity. Globalization threatens both the identities of the original residents of the areas in which newcomers settle and those of the immigrants and their children.[3]

In Great Britain over 10 per cent of the population are immigrants. Many immigrants have moved to this country in the past two or three generations. Amanda Huxtable, who grew up in Great Britain with her Jamaican parents, writes about the impact of migration on her family:

> [M]y father was born in a place called Stone Henge in Jamaica which is quite unusual in St. James. My mother was born in St. Thomas in Jamaica and they came here separately as children. My mother was thirteen. That was in 1963. And my father was seventeen in 1961.
>
> I can't imagine my parents ever feeling British… My mum I think she did probably feel British before she came but when she came she realised she wasn't….
>
> At that time we are talking about the seventies. It was very rare to see anybody of any different colour. You could tell mum and dad used to reminisce and talk about people and things…
>
> I didn't eat anything else other than Jamaican food in my home. My mum used to giggle when I used to come home at six and my mother used to say, 'what did you eat when you were at school?' I'd tell her and she used to laugh her head off. You know, it was the only experience of other food.

As a child I valued Jamaica more than my parents did. That's how I felt. I felt that Jamaica was a place I should be. That I was born here by accident and I didn't belong here. All the racism and bad behaviour from other people wouldn't have been necessary. I should have been born on the island that loved me…Whereas my parents, when I was younger, valued England for what it could give them in terms of economics and better life for their children…

I don't think my father ever felt at home apart from when he was on a cricket field.[4]

1. What skills do citizens need to be able to participate in an informed discussion about immigration and national identity with people whose background and politics are different from their own?

2. If we are a nation of immigrants, how should this influence the way we perceieve newcomers to Great Britain?

3. Below is an example of an identity chart. Using this model, create an identity chart for Amanda Huxtable. What words does she use to describe herself? How would her identity chart be different from her parents'?

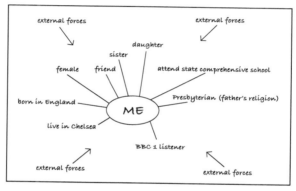

4. What does Huxtable's story suggest about the relationship between immigration and identity? What challenges did she face? How do you explain the differences between her perspective and that of her parents?

---

[1] Mayerlene Frow, *Roots of the Future: Ethnic Diversity in the Making Britain* (London: Commission for Racial Equality, 1997), 9.

[2] Ibid., 8.

[3] Carola Suárez-Orozco, 'Formulating Identity in a Globalized World', *Education and Globalization* (Berkley: University of California Press, 2004), 173.

[4] Amanda Huxtable, 'Migration from a Second Generation Perspective', *Moving Here: 200 Years of Migration to England*. http://www.movinghere.org.uk/stories/Story_YMH_AfroCarib02/Story_YMH_AfroCarib02.htm?identifier=stories/Story_YMH_AfroCarib02/Story_YMH_AfroCarib02.htm&ProjectNo=52 (accessed 14 April 2009).

Teaching Britishness

As the British Empire expanded across the globe into Africa, Asia, Ireland, and North America, its leaders struggled to pass on a British identity to their subjects. Across the Empire, education in British history and literature was seen as essential in those efforts. In a paper submitted to Parliament in 1853, Sir Charles Trevelyan wrote:

> Familiarly acquainted with us by means of our literature, the Indian youth almost cease to regard us as foreigners.... Educated in the same objects engaged in the same pursuits with ourselves, they become more English than Hindoos [sic], just as the Roman provincial became more Roman than Gauls or Italians....The natives will not rise against us, because we shall stoop to raise them.

During the reign of Queen Victoria, leaders began to envision a celebration that would 'remind children that they formed part of the British Empire, and that they might think with others in lands across the sea, what it meant to be sons and daughters of such a glorious Empire.'[1] The idea imagined Queen Victoria, Empress of India, as a figure unifying what was then one quarter of the world's population.

> However it was not until after the death of Queen Victoria, who died on 22 January 1901, that Empire Day was first celebrated. The first 'Empire Day' took place on 24th May 1902, the Queen's birthday. Although not officially recognised as an annual event until 1916, many schools across the British Empire were celebrating it before then. One New Zealand school journal from 1910 records: 'This is the 'Union Jack'; and now that Empire Day has come round once more, you will hear its history. It is really a coloured picture from a history-book, telling of things that happened, long before you were born.'

Each Empire Day, millions of school children from all walks of life across the length and breadth of the British Empire would typically salute the union flag and sing patriotic songs like Jerusalem and God Save the Queen. They would hear inspirational speeches and listen to tales of 'daring do' from across the Empire, stories that included such heroes as Clive of India, Wolfe of Québec and 'Chinese Gordon' of Khartoum. But of course the real highlight of the day for the children was that they were let out of school early in order to take part in the thousands of marches, maypole dances, concerts and parties that celebrated the event.

In Britain an Empire Movement was formed, with its goal in the words of its Irish founder Lord Meath, 'to promote the systematic training of children in all virtues which conduce to the creation of good citizens.' Those virtues were also clearly spelled out by the watchwords of the Empire Movement: 'Responsibility, Sympathy, Duty, and Self-sacrifice.'

Celebrating Commonwealth Day. Empire Day was renamed Commonwealth Day in 1958.

> Empire Day remained an essential part of the calendar for more than 50 years, celebrated by countless millions of children and adults alike, an opportunity to demonstrate pride in being part of the British Empire. By the 1950s, however, the Empire had started to decline, and Britain's relationship with the other countries that formed the Empire had also changed, as they began to celebrate their own identity.[2]

With the decline of the British Empire, immigration to the British mainland increased. While Great Britain has had numerous waves of immigration, these new immigrants arrived in large numbers from former colonies, including the West Indies, and the recently independent South Asian states of India and Pakistan.* No longer united by Empire, the issue of learning to be British took on new meaning. Empire Day was re-named Commonwealth Day, in recognition that the relationship between England and its former colonies had changed. In 1962, 14 years after Windrush, the British government passed its first immigration act, limiting migration from the Commonwealth.

According to the legislation:

> It is clearly important that the flow of immigrants into this densely populated country should not exceed at the rate at which they can be absorbed into the life of the community and properly accommodated in the large cities where work is available; limitation is in the interests of the people of this country, of the immigrants already settled here, and of the new immigrants themselves. …It is evident that many more people from the Commonwealth wish to come to Britain than can possibly be absorbed.

Despite the law, newcomers continued to arrive—first through family re-unification policies that allowed family members of immigrants to obtain citizenship, and later, refugees seeking asylum from persecution and violence made their way to Great Britain.

---

*Bangledesh would become a separate country in 1971.

CONNECTIONS

1. Why do you think colonial leaders wanted to pass along a British identity to their subjects? What did they hope to achieve?

2. How should nations recognize newcomers' cultures and identities? How might they facilitate their peaceful integration?

3. What was the purpose of Empire Day? How does the notion of British identity celebrated during Empire Day differ from British identity today? Why do you think it is different?

4. What arguments did the government make in support of the 1962 immigration act? How is it similar to the debates about today?

5. If you were to create a day-long celebration for a common British identity, what would the celebration look like?

---

[1] '24th May-Empire Day for Queen and the Country!' Historic UK website, http://www.historic-uk.com/HistoryUK/England-History/EmpireDay.htm (accessed 14 April 2009).
[2] Ibid.

THE CRICKET TEST

Amanda Huxtable says that her immigrant parents never really felt at home in Britain. How are people from another country integrated into society? What values are expected to be shared? What differences are accommodated? How much does an individual or a nation allow or encourage the display of allegiance to, or attachment to, culture, nation, or religion? In 1990, Norman Tebbit, a Member of Parliament, suggested a test to measure the loyalty of immigrants. He suggested asking immigrants whom they root for in a cricket match—their former country or Great Britain.

Tebbit speculated that:

> A large proportion of Britain's Asian population fail to pass the cricket test. Which side do they cheer for? It's an interesting test. Are you still harking back to where you came from or where you are?[1]

How is loyalty defined? Mangala Nanda argues that the cricket test is not a good measure of loyalty or Britishness at all:

> I am British. I am also Indian. My family moved to England when I was 14, and I have lived exactly half my life in London. I cheer for India in cricket matches. I claim with pride that Sachin Tendulkar is Indian, and I scream with excitement when Sehwag hits yet another six. Norman Tebbit infers that I must be disloyal to Britain. I disagree. I challenge the very notion of this cricket test. I refuse to accept that an answer to his single question can capture the complexity of what I feel and who I am.
>
> I grew up with a sense of excitement around Indian cricket matches. I remember that big matches were always accompanied with great anticipation at home; my dad and brother in particular would spend ages strategizing about

India's chances versus the opposing team. There was shouting at the TV, painful tension when it looked like we wouldn't make it, elation when our batsmen managed to crank out sixes, and heart wrenching despair when we lost. Neither my brother nor I live at home now, so there aren't often opportunities for us to watch matches together. My parents don't normally subscribe to the sports cable channels either. But sometimes there's a wonderful confluence of events—my brother and I are both home at the same time, and the Indian cricket team is on tour. My parents will fork out the extra £40 to subscribe to Sky Sports for the month—and we watch cricket together. Cheering for India is a special family tradition.

In India, cricket is a religion. People play it on the streets, in their backyards, and in the parks. And everyone plays it—rich people, poor people, south Indians, north Indians, Hindus, Muslims, Sikhs, and more. Whenever I watch a match, I feel the nation's collective excitement. I like to feel that connectedness with India. I don't think that is unreasonable. We are all shaped by the stories of our families, and these inform the things we care about. India is certainly not the only, or the most important, part of me—but my story would be incomplete without it. When I cheer for India, I am not 'harking back to where I was' but acknowledging that there is a part of me that connects to India, today.

The Tebbit test fails to recognize the multi-faceted nature of identity. It forces people into boxes that may not reflect how they see themselves. Those who cheer for the country of their heritage are labeled 'disloyal', while those who choose to support Britain are not. I do feel connection to India, and this is reflected through my support of its cricket team. But I am also deeply connected to Britain, through my engagement with society every single day. I am a socially responsible, politically engaged citizen and I choose to build my life in this country. So I am insulted by Tebbit's assertion that I 'fail' in a test of loyalty. His black and white categorization does not allow me to express how much I love London, my friends, my work, and my life here. Perhaps if Lord Tebbit had engaged me in a conversation rather than a 'test of loyalty', he could have understood this a little better.[2]

Journalist Stephen Pollard believes that the idea of the test can reveal often unspoken assumptions about belonging. In a column for the *Daily Telegraph,* he used the idea of the 'cricket test' to illustrate the way that Jews are often thought of as outsiders.

> Next Wednesday, England play[s] Andorra in a qualification match for the 2008 European Championships. I am rather surprised that nobody has yet asked me which team I want to win. Surprised, because all sorts of people have asked me the same question about England's match tomorrow.
>
> I was born, bred and brought up in London. I have only ever lived in England. …
>
> So why should anyone be in doubt as to which team I want to win tomorrow?
>
> For one reason: I am Jewish, and tomorrow England plays Israel. And although, for most Englishmen, their support for the national football team is a given, for Jews, apparently, it is not.
>
> … I'm an Englishman; I want England to win. But I hear echoes of the Tebbit test when people ask me which team I will be supporting when we play in Tel Aviv tomorrow. They are making (albeit unconsciously) an interesting point. They are assuming that, as a Jew, I am somehow not as English as they are. While their loyalty to the team is implicit, mine is— for no other reason than my Jewishness—open to question.

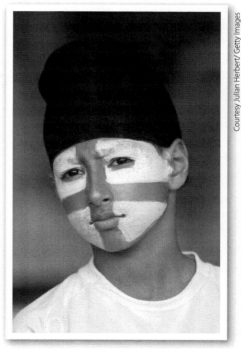

In India, a cricket fan proudly displays his allegiance to England.

Their assumption is based on the latest incarnation of the medieval trope of the Wandering Jew, renewed in the 20th century in Fritz Hippler's 1940 Nazi film, *The Eternal Jew*, and in Stalin's labelling of Jews as 'rootless cosmopolitans.' In such portrayals, Jews remain loyal only to themselves and their tribe, wherever they happen to live, and scheme to undermine the state to their own nefarious ends.

The creation of Israel in 1948 gave this an added twist. Jews are no longer just a rootless tribe conspiring for their own advantage, but are now also agents of a foreign power who use their overweening influence in politics, business and the media to align foreign policy in Israel's interests'...

Jews are not alone in standing accused of being outsiders whose loyalties are not merely split, but are actively devoted to pursuing a foreign power's agenda. When JFK stood for the presidency in 1960, his Roman Catholicism was presented as a barrier to his being a loyal president. Surely he would take instruction from the Vatican? He rebuffed the notion: 'Whatever issue may come before me as President—on birth control, divorce, censorship, gambling, or any other subject—I will make my decision in accordance with what my conscience tells me to be the national interest, and without regard to outside religious pressures or dictates. And no power or threat of punishment could cause me to decide otherwise.'

And many mainstream Muslims, who proudly see themselves as British, have no desire to establish the Caliphate and do not believe there is a contradiction between Islam and Western democracy, suffer a similar bigotry. Attaching such significance to frivolous jokes about split loyalties caused by a football match might seem over the top. But anti-Semitism is resurgent...

[W]hen you ask which team I want to win tomorrow, you are, even if in all innocence, proving my point.[3]

CONNECTIONS

1. Why are some people asked to prove their loyalty while others are not? Why might some minorities feel particularly obligated to prove their loyalty?

2. Tebbit argues that who you cheer for in a cricket match reveals your true loyalty and identity. What are the different components of your identity? Are there times when one part of your identity—age, gender, ethnicity, religion—feels more important than others?

3. Why do you think Stephen Pollard was upset when people asked him what team he was going to root for? For him, what did the questions reveal about antisemitism?

4. What do the selections suggest about the limitations of the Tebbit test as a way to explore identity?

---

[1] Darcus Howe, 'Tebbit's loyalty test is dead', *New Statesmen*, 3 July, 2006, http://www.newstatesman.com/200607030029 (accessed 20 March 2009).
[2] Mangala Nanda 'Rethinking the Cricket Test', (working paper, 20 March 2009).
[3] Stephan Pollard, 'Am I Doubted Because I'm a Jew?' *Telegraph*, 6 January 2009, http://www.telegraph.co.uk/comment/personal-view/3638653/Am-I-doubted-because-Im-a-Jew.html (accessed 14 April 2009).

RELIGION AND BELONGING

Migrants and strangers, anthropologists warn us, do not come with labels; instead they are often created as a minority by a majority that lays claim to the social or national 'we.' Journalist Sarfraz Manzoor writes that many Asians in Britain have recently defined themselves less by ethnic and national culture, and more by religion:

> The term Asian was coined in 1948 by British administrators working in colonial Kenya to describe citizens of newly independent India and Pakistan. It was brought into this country 20 years later with the arrival of Kenyan Asians....
>
> Pakistanis, Indians and Bangladeshis realised that it was an expedient phrase but Asian continued to gain mainstream currency with the success of films such as *East is East* and programmes like *Goodness Gracious Me*.
>
> It became cool to be Asian. Despite its fragile origins, Asian seemed to be solidifying into something that was clear, distinct, and tangible.
>
> It took a catastrophe to remind us that the word obscured as much as it illuminated, and to expose just how much it hid. The impact of 9/11 on the US and international security is well known. Less noticed has been its impact on Britain's Asian communities. Among the first victims of violence after the attacks on New York and Washington were not Muslims but Sikhs, targeted for their prominent beards and turbans. September 11 changed the type and nature of racial abuse— instead of 'Paki' the new term of abuse became 'Bin Laden' and 'al-Qaida', and the abuse was motivated not by race, but by religion. Hindus and Sikhs, frustrated at being mistaken for Muslims, resolved to assert their own religious identity. In doing so they were sending a message to the rest of the country: we had nothing to do with terrorism and riots—that's the work of those trouble-making Muslims.

For the Muslims, September 11 prompted a resurgence of interest in Islam with many choosing to embrace their religion as a response to seeing their community vilified and demonised.

… If Muslims, Hindus and Sikhs are defining themselves by their religion, does it matter to anyone outside these communities?

And this is the critical question. Is this new religious identity part of an overarching plural identity, or is it exclusive and separate? Put more bluntly, it is a choice between either wanting religion to be a part of an identity or only being defined by religion and arguing that it is more important than any national identity.[1]

Courtesy Sion Touhig/ Corbis

Here, a Muslim girl visibly shows her religion by wearing a hijab headscarf. After the 9/11 attacks, many Muslims notably embraced their religion in response to the defamatory statements about their community.

Like Mazoor, Yasmin Hai is a Pakistani Muslim who writes about religion and belonging. She and many Asians of her generation were encouraged to assimilate, but many struggled to fit in. Hai writes about her friend Nazia who used religion as a way to define herself against a British society that would not accept her:

> When my friend Nazia started flirting with Islam, I felt betrayed. Over the years, we had been clubbing together and got up to all sorts of mischief. Now she was abandoning me.
>
> I wasn't bothered that she'd started praying five times a day. . . . But when she started denigrating Western culture, I felt that she'd betrayed me, herself and our entire Asian community.
>
> I'd grown up in suburban Wembley in a strongly Asian area. My father, who had come to Britain from Pakistan as a political refugee in 1964, was ambitious for his family. So he encouraged my younger brother and sister and me to adopt the ways of the English.
>
> We were banned, for example, from speaking Urdu to our mother: she could speak to us in our mother tongue, but we had to answer in English. Nor were we encouraged to practise Islam. In fact, my father bought me the Book of Common Prayer so I wouldn't feel excluded during school assemblies.
>
> Most of my friends were brought up in similar culturally ambiguous households. So when my friend Nazia started using racist terminology, stereotyping white people as cultureless drunks who don't know how to look after their children, I was furious.
>
> We had both gone to university; but while I flourished at Manchester and threw myself into the club scene, she was finding the normal excesses of university life unsettling. It was then that she started to feel that she would never be able to participate fully in English life. After graduating, she agreed to an arranged marriage—her way of reconnecting with the Asian community. But when the marriage failed, the community ostracised her.

This rejection was devastating. At that point, she started to take an interest in the more politicised version of Islam that had begun to filter through in the early 1990s.

Becoming a strict Muslim was her way of exacting revenge on the community that had deserted her when she needed it most.

She wasn't the only one I knew to take that path. For so many of my Asian friends, radical Islam was not so much a matter of being anti-West as a way of wresting back some form of identity. In the early 1990s, many of them had thrown themselves into the club and drug scene. Most, though, eventually started to suffer from a creeping form of cultural guilt.

Becoming a committed Muslim was a way of being born again, of wiping the slate clean. You could use your new identity to define yourself against the Western way of life—and against your parents.

As many of us weren't fluent in our mother tongue, and often discouraged from talking about our problems, we hadn't ever had a meaningful dialogue with our parents. My own relationship with my mother suffered immeasurably as a result of this.

. . . At the heart of the disillusionment that many of my friends felt was not knowing how they fitted into British society. I wasn't immune, either. At 19, I found myself becoming increasingly drawn to Islam. I was struck, when I visited Pakistan, by the confidence of the people, who seemed comfortable in their own skins in a way that my friends and I were not.

Here, the chasm that now exists between Asian generations has created a generation of vulnerable young people seeking direction and a sense of belonging. And that makes them more likely to turn to a fundamentalist ideology that professes to offer answers.

. . . In my own case, I realised eventually that I didn't have to force my life into a narrative that had been imposed on it by either British—or radical…conventional wisdoms. There was nothing wrong with being me.[2]

Hai, like most of her peers was able to find a comfortable balance between religion and national identity. Manzoor explains:

> How you define yourself tells others a lot about you and who you think you are. Britain's Hindus, Sikhs, and Muslims were long defined by others in terms of what they were not: not white, not black, not British. Now, for the first time, identities are being forged from inside the communities and with confidence. These identities emphasise religion but do not necessarily imply disloyalty to being British.
>
> The great danger, however, is that an identity that emboldens the individual can also threaten the wider society. The challenge to ensure that does not happen is one that affects all Britons—be they Christian, Hindu, Sikh or Muslim.[3]

CONNECTIONS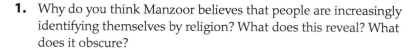

1. Why do you think Manzoor believes that people are increasingly identifying themselves by religion? What does this reveal? What does it obscure?

2. Manzoor asks, 'If Muslims, Hindus and Sikhs are defining themselves by their religion, does it matter to anyone outside these communities?' How would you answer that question?

3. Manzoor talks about the way Hindus and Sikhs started to highlight their differences from Muslims in the aftermath of the terrorist attacks. Why do you think some of them did this? How did the environment shape the way people started to define their identity? How has the environment shaped the way you define yourself?

4. Hai writes, 'becoming a committed Muslim was a way of being born again, of wiping the slate clean.' Why might some young people want to wipe the slate clean?

5. What insights does Hai offer about her generation's search for identity? How does she reconcile her two identities?

---

[1] Sarfraz Manzoor, 'We've ditched race for religion', *The Guardian*, 11 January, 2005, http://www.guardian.co.uk/world/2005/jan/11/race.religion (accessed 15 April 2009).

[2] Yasmin Hai, 'Revenge of young Muslims', *The Sunday Times*, 6 April 2008, http://www.timesonline.co.uk/tol/comment/columnists/guest_contributors/article3689767.ece (accessed 14 April 2009).

[3] Manzoor, Ibid.

Accommodating Differences

Here, Asian and African-American children gather outside a pub displaying the Cross of St. George.

The efforts to integrate diverse populations often raise questions about how far societies should go to accommodate minorities. These civic dilemmas are often hotly debated on the streets and in the press.

Some people believe the best way to integrate newcomers into British society is to immerse them into British culture as they previously learned it. They believe that too much accommodation of differences will limit opportunities for individuals, and harm the national interest in the long run. One of them is British writer and psychiatrist Anthony Daniels. He writes under the pen name Theodore Dalrymple. The grandson of immigrants, Daniels argues that Britain has stopped doing many of the things that might make it possible for his father to assimilate into British culture and society:

[O]ne can take the driver's licence test in Britain in a startling variety of languages. Spoken instructions come even in the various dialects of Albanian, Kurdish, and Lingala. For the written part, test takers need not know how to read the Latin alphabet (that would be discriminatory): officials provide the questions in the script of your choice. Never mind that traffic signs are still in English.

Nor is the driver's test anomalous. Government pamphlets, including those concerning health and social-security benefits, now routinely appear in myriad languages—at public expense. When I went to vote in the local elections not long ago, I saw notices in various Indian languages and in Vietnamese explaining how to cast a vote. And at my local airport, the sign directing travelers to the line for returning British passport holders is written not only in English, but in Bengali, Hindi, Punjabi, and Urdu (each with its own script): proof that the granting of citizenship requires no proficiency in the national language.

These practices send the message that newcomers to Britain have no obligation to learn English… British officialdom doubtless does not know that the confusion of languages after the Tower of Babel fell was meant as a punishment….

My family history attests… to British society's generous capacity to absorb. My father, whose immigrant parents never learned to speak English well, attended a slum school during and just after World War I, with classmates so poor that they went hungry and barefoot. Despite his background, my father found himself inducted into British culture by teachers who did not believe that the ability to understand and appreciate Milton or Shakespeare, or to make a contribution to national life, depended on social class, or required roots in the soil going back before the Norman conquest. His teachers had the same faith in the liberating power of high culture, in its universal value and appeal, that many British workers then shared…

My father's teachers were the only people I ever heard him mention with unqualified admiration and gratitude…They had no desire to enclose my father in the world that his parents had fled. And they understood that for society to avoid bitter internal conflicts, everyone had to share important elements of culture and historical knowledge that would result in a shared identity…Not to teach Shakespeare or other giants of British culture is to provide no worthwhile tradition with which the increasingly diverse population can identify….

It simply never occurred to anyone in my father's day that the children of immigrants should or would have a fundamentally different culture from that of the larger population, or that they would have any cultural peculiarities or sensibilities that needed catering to. They would be British without qualification. These immigrants, of course, arrived during a prolonged era of national self-confidence, when Britain was either a rising or a risen power. The generosity of my father's teachers grew out of pride in their culture and country.

A new mass immigration to Britain from every region of the globe, in which the differences between the immigrants and the host population are profound, has occurred precisely at the moment when the multiculturalists have helped undermine the capacity of British culture to absorb them….

Recently, a highly intelligent Iranian refugee consulted me. The medical part of the consultation over, we began to chat about Iranian affairs…He appreciated deeply the British institutions that now protected him. He had experienced occasional hostility from individual Britons, but he realized that it was the product of ineradicable human nature, not of official malice. Above all, he said, Britain had a different history from Iran's—of struggle no doubt, but also of compromise—which allowed us to take our liberty for granted (a dangerous thing to do). It was, he said, a very valuable and inspiring history. What impressed him first when he arrived was how everyone just assumed that he could say what he liked, without fear of retribution—a freedom above price. But he recognized that he could only be part of that worthy society if he chose to fit in, abandoning any aspects of his Iranian culture incompatible with it, which he was only too happy to do. The fundamental demands and responsibilities, he felt, were upon the immigrant, not upon the host country.[1]

How should schools balance the need to create a common identity among their students and at the same time respect the different religious and cultural backgrounds of the student population? Finding the right balance is hard work. One British school found itself in the middle of controversy when officials decided to accommodate a growing Muslim population by serving only meat that has been slaughtered according to halal [Islamic dietary law]. While some parents support the changes, a number of parents demonstrated in opposition. A mother of a student at the school explained her position:

> 'I sent my kids to this school because I don't want them to be affected by religion….We can't force our culture on someone else because that's not right so we shouldn't have someone else's culture forced on us…. The little culture that we have is being lost….'
>
> She added: 'I totally deny being guilty of racism. We allow people to come into this country and we end up being in a minority. We accommodate other cultures at the expense of ours.'[2]

CONNECTIONS

1. Do nations need an historical narrative that all newcomers need to adopt? How do those narratives change? Who writes the historical narratives of a nation? How are they taught?

2. Create an identity chart for Great Britain. What words, images, and phrases would you include? How would that identity chart compare to charts representing Great Britain 50 years ago? One hundred years ago? Three hundred years ago? (See the reading 'An Island of Immigrants' for an example of an identity chart.)

3. How do the identities of nations change over time? How are those identities expressed publically?

4. Why are some people concerned that recognizing newcomers' identities can threaten national identity?

5. Daniels believes that people in Britain have stopped doing many of the things that allow immigrants to integrate in British society. He writes:

> It simply never occurred to anyone in my father's day that the children of immigrants should or would have a fundamentally different culture from that of the larger population, or that they would have any cultural peculiarities or sensibilities that needed catering to.

6. To what extent does recognizing and accomodating cultural, linguistic, and religious differences facilitate intergration? To what extent might accomodating differences hinder integration?

7. How did the administrators at the school try to accommodate differences? What do you think of the school's decision to serve only halal meat in the cafeteria? How might you have handled the situation?

8. How does the mother quoted in the excerpt explain her decision to protest the cafeteria's policy? If you were a school official, how might you try to resolve the conflict?

---

[1] Theodore Dalrymple, 'Multiculturalism Starts Losing Its Luster', *City Journal* (Summer 2004) http://www.city-journal.org/html/14_3_oh_to_be.html (accessed 14 April 2009).

[2] 'Parents protest at school's 'Halal-only' lunch', *Daily Mail*, 9 February 2007, http://www.dailymail.co.uk/pages/live/articles/news/news.html?in_article_id=435198&in_page_id=1770 (accessed 6 October 2009).

Turning Points

Billy Bragg grew up in Barking, a white working class neighborhood in the East End of London at a time when anti-immigrant feeling was high.

Back in the late 70s, I was working in an office, a place of casual racism and homophobia. I never spoke out against it because I felt I was in a minority and didn't want the grief. On the streets, the National Front were marching through immigrant neighborhoods, stirring up trouble and trying to divide communities.

I may well have carried on turning a blind eye were it not for the Clash. When their name was added to the bill of the first Rock Against Racism carnival in April 1978, I knew I had to be there. When I arrived at the rally, in east London, I was amazed to see 100,000 young people just like me—one for every vote the National Front had won in the council elections the year before.

I came away with a strong sense that this was where my generation was going to make its stand. Just as youth in the 50s had marched against the bomb, and the long-hairs of the 60s had opposed the Vietnam War, we were going to define ourselves in opposition to discrimination in all its forms.

Rock Against Racism was a watershed in the development of multiculturalism in this country…. We fought the narrow-mindedness of the National Front by widening our cultural horizons….

Well, it was the music of the Clash that got me to the Rock Against Racism carnival. However, it wasn't the songs they played that day, or the speeches that were made from the stage that changed my world. It was being in that audience. I went to work the next day determined to speak up against the racists, confident in the knowledge that I was not alone.[1]

Bragg took the festival's message of tolerance to the stage with him as he became a successful musician. In recent years, Bragg has found a new outlet for his ideas. He has published a book, and now writes a weekly newspaper column. With words and music, Bragg promotes his vision of 'progressive patriotism'—a vision of an inclusive English identity that is not threatened by diversity.

In one of his columns he explained:

Over the past few years there has been a growing sense of victimhood among sections of the indigenous population, a feeling that, although in the majority, white Britons are somehow being oppressed. This... idea is often expressed in radio phone-ins where disgruntled callers claim they 'are no longer allowed to be British.' I listen intently as the host asks them to identify who, exactly, is denying them their right to be British, and in what way.[2]

Courtesy Tibor Bozi/ Corbis

As a young adult Bragg remembers a transformation of sorts—a turning point in his life—when he gained the courage to speak out against intolerance.

Bragg suggests that the solution is to take pride in English history and identity, and to share it in a way that helps build connections to newcomers:

> But does our history—that of a white, Christian, democratic society—have anything to say to those who have recently arrived from countries that share none of these characteristics? Can heritage accommodate those who feel excluded? I believe it can.
>
> Less than a century ago, most British citizens were excluded from fully realising their individual potential by class barriers; excluded from expressing their democratic will by gender; excluded from good health by poverty. All the way back to the Magna Carta, our history has examples of people standing up for their right to be treated fairly. It is this struggle for belonging that connects the majority of English people with the minority of recently arrived immigrants—a struggle to be accepted as part of society, as respected, responsible citizens.
>
> Our history, far from being a stuffy subject that concerns itself merely with kings, queens, and generals, has the potential to make an important contribution to the increasingly fractious debate about who does and does not belong. To counter those who exploit fear in order to divide communities, we urgently need to highlight the common threads that bind us as a society. First and foremost will be the country that we share: the 'English' in English heritage is surely a matter of place, not race.[3]

CONNECTIONS ◆ ◆ ◆ ◆ ◆ ◆ ◆ ◆ ◆

1. Bragg remembers the Rock Against Racism concert as a turning point that gave him the confidence to speak out against racism. Have you ever had a turning point that changed the way you thought about an issue or one that gave you the confidence to stand up against injustice?

2. Bragg's story begins with his memory of ignoring racist comments at work. What do you and your friends do when you hear stereotypes, racist remarks, or ethnic jokes? How do you decide whether to say something or let the moment pass? If you have ever spoken out, what did you say? If you ignored the racist remark, why did you choose to remain silent? In either case, how did you feel about your decision later? What effect did it have on you and others? How important are those moments?

3. Bragg fears that with increased diversity, some white Britons feel that they are being left out, and they 'are no longer allowed to be British.' What do you think they mean? How does he propose to help them feel included in the changes that are taking place?

4. When can expressions of group identity be constructive? Why do some people find expressions of group identity threatening?

[1] Billy Bragg, 'The Day I realised music could change the world', *The Guardian*, 8 October, 2007, http://www.guardian.co.uk/uk/2007/oct/08/race.music (accessed 14 April 2009).

[2] Billy Bragg, 'They're not just British values but we need them anyway', *The Guardian*, 10 April, 2007, http://www.guardian.co.uk/commentisfree/2007/apr/10/comment.politics/print (accessed 14 April 2009).

[3] Billy Bragg, 'The struggle for belonging' *The Guardian*, 7 November, 2006, http://www.guardian.co.uk/commentisfree/2006/nov/07/comment.homeaffairs (accessed 14 April 2009).

FITTING IN

Adolescence is a time when many young people are in the process of defining their own identities. One of the ways that adolescents define themselves is through the groups to which they belong. In this story, Shane Meadows, a filmmaker, recalls his own search to 'fit in.' He was a skinhead before the movement became associated with the promotion of white power, violence, and racism towards ethnic minorities. In the 1980s, as the economic situation in Britain worsened, many skinheads were linked with the National Front, a political party which wanted to curtail non-white immigration into Great Britain, and send ethnic minorities 'home,' Meadows explored his experiences in the film *This is England*.

Set in 1983, [This is England] is the first period film I have made. A great deal of it is based on my own childhood and I tried to re-create my memories of being an 11-year-old kid trying to fit in…. Like most 11-year-old kids who wore jumpers with animals on, I got bullied by the older kids at school. So I looked for my own tribe to join. It was the skinhead movement that enamoured me the most. I remember seeing 10 or 15 of them at the bus shelter on my way home from school one summer night and thinking they were the most fearsome thing I had ever seen. Even though I was terrified of them, I was instantly attracted to them. To be a part of most of the other factions, you had to be a little rich kid. But to be a skinhead, all you needed was a pair of jeans, some work boots, a white shirt and a shaved head. You could be transformed from a twerp into a fearsome warrior in 15 minutes. Skins appealed to me because they were like soldiers: they wore their outfits like suits of armour and demanded respect. There were playground myths that surrounded them and especially their Dr Martens boots. It was feared that a single kick from a DM boot would kill you or at the very least give you brain damage. I can remember kids refusing to fight unless the skinhead agreed to remove his fearsome boots first.

British Skinheads in the 1980s. Filmmaker Shane Meadows explains that the National Front were able to recruit many frustrated Skinheads into their movement.

My older sister was going out with a skinhead who took me under his wing and taught me about the roots of the whole culture. He was a nice bloke who bore no relation to the stereotypical racist yob that people now associate with that time. I learned from him that skinheads had grown out of working class English lads working side by side with West Indians in factories and shipyards in the late 60s. The black lads would take the whites to blues parties where they were exposed to ska music for the first time. Soon, Jamaican artists like Desmond Dekker, the Upsetters and Toots and The Maytals were making a living out of songs aimed directly at English white kids. This was where the whole skinhead thing came from—it was inherently multicultural.

But nowadays when I tell people that I used to be a skinhead, they think I'm saying I used to be racist. My film shows how rightwing politics started to creep into skinhead culture in the 1980s and change people's perception of it. This was a time when there were three and a half million people unemployed and we were involved in a pointless war in the Falklands. When people are frustrated and disillusioned, that's when you get extremist groups moving in and trying to exploit the situation. That's what the National Front did in the early 80s. Skinheads had always taken pride in being working class and English, so they were easy targets for the National Front who said that their identities were under threat. They cultivated a real hatred of the Asian community. [The National Front used] charismatic leaders to turn skinheads into violent street enforcers. Suddenly, all skinheads were branded the same way. But most of the real old skins who were into the music and the clothes went on to be scooter boys to separate themselves from the racism. I always wanted 'This Is England' to tell the truth about skinheads.[1]

While many skinheads rejected racism, Meadows also talks about his skinhead friend who identified with the National Front. This friend was represented by the character Combo in the film:

He was a very bright kid at 21, but was basically claiming to be a racist. I don't think he was. I don't think he actually believed it, but I think he wanted something to blame, and to belong to. He'd…go to quite a few of those [National Front] meetings seen in the film. The sort of people who came out of the woodwork at these meetings weren't just skinheads, they'd be local farmers who'd come down. If you're from a really small place, with virtually no Asian, Chinese, or black community, it's very easy from reading a few headlines to think there's this massive problem.[2]

CONNECTIONS ◆ ◆ ◆ ◆ ◆ ◆ ◆ ◆ ◆

1. What initially attracted Meadows to the skinhead movement? What did belonging to the skinheads offer a young person like Meadows?

2. How does Meadows explain why racism began to 'creep into skinhead culture'? What factors does he cite?

3. Why might tough economic times make some people more vulnerable to the kind of solutions offered by the National Front? What did National Front leaders do to recruit young people to join their movement?

4. Why do you think young people might join a group that advocates hatred and violence? How does Meadows explain why his friend joined the National Front?

5. If a friend of yours started to become attracted to a group that promotes hate, what can you do or say that might convince them that they were making a bad choice?

6. What is similar about the rise of racism within the skinhead movement to what you know about other extremist groups? What is different?

---

[1] Shane Meadows, 'Under My Skin', *The Guardian*, 21 April 2007, http://www. guardian.co.uk/film/2007/apr/21/culture.features (accessed 14 April 2009).
[2] Shane Meadows, 'Shane Meadows on *This Is England*', Channel 4 http://www. channel4.com/film/reviews/feature.jsp?id=160615 (accessed 14 April 2009).

LESSONS IN BELONGING

Image of a main street in Bury Park located in the town of Luton which is north of London.

In his memoir *Greetings from Bury Park,* Sarfraz Manzoor writes about the experiences—in and out of school—that shaped his understanding of what it means to be British.

> My father left Pakistan when he was twenty-nine but he never stopped being Pakistani. He came to Britain for economic reasons and his relationship to this country remained rooted in financial pragmatism rather than emotional attachment. 'This is not your country,' he would tell me, 'you have to have your own language'. I was brought up to believe that Pakistan was our true home and Britain merely where we happened to live. When we lived in Bury Park, it was an easy distinction to maintain; we lived around mostly Pakistanis, I went to a school that was mostly Pakistani and the only people who ever visited our home were Pakistanis. When we moved to Marsh Farm,

that all changed. At school I was just another schoolboy collecting Panini football stickers and stealing peeks at the girls doing handsprings in their knickers, but at home my parents were constantly reminding me I was Pakistani and different from my friends….

On the way to Lea Manor [his school], there was a subway where a gang of skinheads would hang out. They looked like glue sniffers and I knew they were trouble: a Sikh boy called Rupinder, who was one year below me at school, had told me of how the boys had spat on him as he tried to walk through the underpass. After he told me this story, I was always nervous about seeing the skinheads and changed my route to school. Not all racists were so easily identifiable. When I asked someone, for example, where the nearest bus stop was, and the lad pointed me in the wrong direction, I would know he was a racist: racists loved giving bad directions.

At Lea Manor there were very few Asian pupils and only one Asian teacher. His name was Mr Judge and he taught maths. Mr Judge was a short, plump, middle-aged man who wore a large turban, thick glasses and dressed in a brown suit, usually over a patterned sweater. Mr Judge's maths lessons were anarchic; each time he turned his back towards us, there would be a flurry of conkers hurled toward him. He vainly tried to discipline us, but his thick Asian accent meant no one took him seriously. Those of us who obeyed Mr Judge did so as much out of sympathy as respect….

As we filed out of the room at the end of our maths lesson, I would see him tidying up his papers and rubbing the equations from the blackboard in advance of another class and, most likely, another grueling hour, and I used to wonder what it must have been like to be Mr Judge. But it wasn't only pupils who could be hurtful. In woodwork, if I got my measurements wrong, the teacher would say, 'I said five centimetres, not five chapattis.'

Another teacher who I was convinced was racist, began one lesson with a discussion about how words could be abbreviated. 'So, for example, you, Sarfraz,' he said, turning to me. I immediately began to feel the tingle of unwanted attention. 'Now, you are Pakistani, are you not?'

'Yes, sir,' I replied.

'So if someone was [sic] to call you a Paki, and the term is a common shorthand for Pakistani, then it would be true to say you are a Paki, would it not?'

I could hear tittering in the class.

'Yes, but no sir...it's not just a shorter word, is it, sir...' I said, trying to make my point.

'All I'm saying, Sarfraz, is that technically, and only technically, mind, you are a Paki...would you agree?'

I looked straight at him. The more smug he looked, the more I hated him. 'Yes sir,' I replied finally.

It is not easy to convey the impact of such incidents...

'What you have to remember,' my father would tell me, 'is that the whites don't actually want you in this country. You do understand that, don't you?...The reason I want you to speak Urdu and not forget you are Pakistani is that you never know when we might have to leave. It could happen. And if it does what will you do? If the Tories say they want to throw us all out, send us back home as they say, what will you do? Do you think your friends...will stand up for you? Take you into their home? Of course they won't. That's why I still keep our house in Pakistan. Open your ears when I tell you this: Pakistan is the only country that will never deny you. It is the only country that you can always call home.'

My father was always dismissive of my friends, I'm not sure he believed it was possible to be friends with a white person. But I knew differently. Scott was my best friend and he was white....

I wished me and Scott could have been actual brothers. If I could have summoned a genie who could have rubbed my brownness off, the shameful truth is that I would have been elated. As that was impossible, I settled on being invisible. That was how I felt being Pakistani in the eighties: I wanted to be invisible and anonymous so that no one could point at me and say: 'You are different and you do not belong.'[1]

CONNECTIONS ◆ ◆ ◆ ◆ ◆ ◆ ◆ ◆ ◆

1. In this excerpt, Manzoor shares several stories that have an impact upon the way he thought about belonging. Considering the impact of these stories, create an identity chart for Manzoor. What factors does he suggest shaped the way he thought about his identity?

2. How do you explain the differences in the way Manzoor and his father thought about their relationship to Britain? How is the way they think about British identity similar and different from those of others you have read in this collection?

3. Experiences at school often have a lasting impact on the way people think about their identities. After describing two painful memories from his school days, Manzoor writes, 'It is not easy to convey the impact of such incidents.' What does he mean? What are the different ways such experiences might shape the way people think about themselves, others, and the choices they make?

4. How do you explain the fact that none of Manzoor's fellow students defended either him or the Asian math teacher when they were teased? What choices did his classmates have in the different situations? What might you have done to help?

5. As a young man Mazoor remembers:

> If I could have summoned a genie who could have rubbed my browness off, the shameful truth is that I would have been elated…I wanted to be invisible and anonymous so that no one could point at me and say: 'You are different and you do not belong.'

What does he mean when he says he wanted to be 'invisible'?

6. Throughout his memoir *Greetings from Bury Park*, Manzoor emphasizes the important role his friends—including white friends—played in his life. How do your friendships shape your sense of belonging? Why might his friendship to Scott have been particularly important for him?

---

[1] Sarfraz Manzoor, *Greetings from Bury Park: A Memoir* (New York: Vintage Books, 2007), 240–55.

ALIENATION

A crucial part of adolescence is a search for identity. For many adolescents, the pressures both from within and outside of their community present tough choices. Religion is an important and often positive component of a developing identity that can provide a framework of values, a sense of belonging, and direction to many adolescents as they navigate their environment. For some young Muslim adolescents in Great Britain, coming to terms with what it means to be in a religious minority can be particularly difficult when they do not feel accepted by society.

Ed Husain, author of *The Islamist*, grew up in a middle class immigrant family in London. In his memoir, he traces his path from primary school in the multicultural East End to his years at university as a religious extremist. Today he has started a foundation to challenge extremism and to integrate Muslims into British society. His story highlights key moments in his childhood that would ultimately shape the choices that he made.

> Growing up in Britain in the 1980s was not easy. Looking back, I think [my teacher] Ms Powlesland was trying to create her own little world of goodwill and kindness for the children in her care. We grew up oblivious of the fact that large numbers of us were somehow different—we were 'Asian.' The warmth of the English fishermen in Upnor did not exist in the streets of east London.
>
> 'Pakis! Pakis! F— off back home!' the hoodlums would shout. The National Front [a nationalist party] was at its peak in the 1980s. I can still see a gang of shaven-headed tattooed thugs standing tall above us, hurling abuse as we walked to the local library to return our books. Ms Powlesland and the other teachers raced to us, held our hands firmly, and roared at the hate-filled bigots.

'Go away! Leave us alone,' they would bellow to taunts of 'Paki lovers' from the thugs. Little did I know then that one day, I, too, would be filled with abhorrence of others.

The colour-blind humanity of most of my teachers, strength in the face of tyranny, taught us lessons for the rest of our lives. Britain was our home, we were children of this soil, and no amount of intimidation would change that—we belonged here. And yet, lurking in the background were forces that were preparing to seize the hearts and minds of Britain's Muslim children.

I was the eldest of four, with a younger brother and twin sisters. My father was born in British India, my mother in East Pakistan [now Bangladesh], and we children in Mile End. My father arrived in England as a young man in 1961 and spent his early days as a restaurateur in Chertsey, Surrey. In ethnic terms I consider myself Indian. . . . Somewhere in my family line there is also Arab ancestry; some say from Yemen and others the Hijaz, a mountainous tract of land along the Red Sea coast in Arabia. This mixed heritage of being British by birth, Asian by descent, and Muslim by conviction was set to tear me apart later in life.

I remember my father used to buy us fresh cakes from a Jewish baker in Brick Lane. Our Koran school building had inherited mezuzahs on the door panels, which our Muslim teachers forbade us from removing out of respect for Judaism. My birthday, a family event at our home, is on Christmas Day. My mother would take us to see Santa Claus every year after [the] school Christmas party. We made a snowman in our garden, lending it my mother's scarf. Opposite our childhood home in Limehouse, a three-storey Victorian terrace, stood Our Lady Immaculate Catholic Church with a convent attached. We were friends of the sisters; our car was parked beside the nunnery every night. We helped out in the church's annual jumble sale. There was never any question of religious tension, no animosity between people of differing faiths. My mother still speaks fondly of her own childhood friends, many of whom were Hindu. But as I grew older, all that changed. The live-and-let-live world of my childhood was snatched away. . . .

It was a school rule that each term we were divided into dining groups of six; we lunched together and laid the table on a rota system. One day I forgot that it was my turn to help set the cutlery. Mr Coppin, mustachioed and blue-eyed, came into the dining hall and grabbed me by the arm. Taking me aside, he lowered his face to mine and yelled, 'Why didn't you set the table?'

'I forgot, Mr Coppin,' I whimpered.

'Forgot? How dare you forget?' he shouted, his hands resting on his knees. 'You're in trouble, young man! Do you understand?'

'Yes, Mr Coppin,' I said.

Then he said something that I have never forgotten. Of me, a nine-year-old, he asked, 'Where is your Allah now then, eh? Where is he? Can't he help you?'

What was he talking about? I wondered. What did Allah have to do with it? Besides, I did not even know precisely who Allah was. I knew Allah was something to do with Islam, but then I also wondered if Islam and Aslan from *The Lion, the Witch, and the Wardrobe* were in any way linked. After Mr Coppin's outburst, I thought it wiser not to ask.

Months before I left Sir William Burrough, I had an accident on the school playground. I fell off a bike and cut my chin. Immediately Cherie, a teacher in whose classroom proudly hung a photo of her standing beside a waxwork of Margaret Thatcher at Madame Tussaud's [wax museum], rushed to help me. She drove me to hospital and held my hand throughout the entire ordeal of stitches and after-care. As we stepped out of the hospital building, she asked me if I wanted a piggy back. Thinking it was some sort of boiled sweet, I happily agreed.

Then, to my bewilderment, she went down on all fours and told me to climb on. I still remember her straightening her dungaree straps, and pushing back her glasses before taking off with me, an eleven-year-old Asian boy with a huge plaster on his chin, clinging on for dear life. Cherie drove me home and showered me with love and care in the days that followed.

> That experience with Cherie, a white, non-Muslim teacher, and the commitment of Ms Powlesland and her staff to me and other pupils at Sir William Burrough, stayed in my mind. It helped me form a belief in Britain, an unspoken appreciation of its values of fairness and equality. It would take me more than a decade to understand what drove Ms Powlesland and Cherie. I was fortunate to have such marvelous teachers at a young age. For later in life, when I doubted my affinity with Britain, those memories came rushing back.[1]

What happens to young people who feel their identities are rejected by the larger society? Psychiatrist James Gilligan, author of *Preventing Violence: Prospects for Tomorrow*, warns that feelings of shame and humiliation are a key factor in understanding violence. He explains, 'I have yet to see a serious act of violence that was not provoked by the experience of feeling shamed and humiliated, disrespected, and ridiculed, and that did not represent the attempt to prevent or undo this 'loss of face'—no matter how severe the punishment, even if it includes death.'[2]

Courtesy Sion Touhig/ Corbis

A British Bengali Teenager in Whitechapel, East London.

CONNECTIONS

1. See Connections in reading 'Island of Immigrants' for an example of an identity chart. Using this model, create two identity charts for Ed Husain—one before Husain is taunted by his teacher and one after his teacher takes him to the hospital. How do those experiences shape Husain's identity? What did he learn from those experiences?

2. Compare Husain's story to that of Sarfraz Manzoor in the reading 'Lessons in Belonging.' What is similar about the two stories? What are the differences?

3. James Gilligan believes that shame and humiliation are key factors in understanding why people behave violently. Why do you think those feelings are so powerful? How might they be different tfrom other emotions?

4. Not everyone who has been shamed or humiliated lashes out in violence. What other factors do you think lead to violence? Why are some people better able to deal with feelings of shame and humiliation than others?

---

[1] Ed Husain, *The Islamist: Why I Joined Radical Islam in Britain, What I Saw Inside and Why I Left* (London: Penguin Books, 2007), 1–5.
[2] James Gilligan, *Violence: Reflections on a National Epidemic* (New York: Vintage Books, 1996), 110.

NOT IN MY NAME

The debates on integration took on new meaning when terrorists organized bomb explosions in two locations of London's transport system—at King's Cross tube station, and on a bus during the middle of the morning commute on 7 July 2005. The perpetrators, young British Muslims, three of whom were of Pakistani descent, justified the atrocities in the name of their religion. For Sarfraz Manzoor, the attacks were personal; he too was a British Muslim from Pakistan. In fact, he had even grown up in the same town, Luton, as one of the bombers. Despite their shared background, Manzoor explains, 'What they felt and what they preached was not in my name.'

> On the morning of 7 July 2005, I was in my flat in London. I awoke and stumbled into the kitchen to make myself a coffee before going into my study and turning on my laptop to check my emails. I had set the BBC news website as my internet homepage, and the top story said that there were some severe power cuts on the London Underground that were causing chaos for morning commuters. One of the greatest pleasures of working from home was the smugness I felt on days when Underground workers went on strike or when signaling failures crippled the tube. It felt so liberating to not have to worry about how to get to work.
>
> Leaving my computer on, I went to my living room and turned on Sky News. They reported that the problems on the Underground were not to do with power cuts, as had been first thought, but were something far more serious. The same sick feeling I had felt four years earlier when I had heard about the attack on the twin towers returned, the same silent pleading that this would not have been perpetrated by Muslims, not again.
>
> When the details began to emerge, it was even worse than I had feared. Four British Muslims, three of them Pakistani, had become Britain's first domestic suicide bombers, and they had set off to London from Luton train station. The same train

station that I used every time I came home to see my family, the same train station my father had dropped me at the last time I had seen him alive. The photograph that the newspapers printed that week of four bombers, with their explosive rucksacks on their backs, was taken at Luton train station as they were about to board the Thameslink train to King's Cross. I knew intimately the route the four men had taken. And, yet again, it was my hometown that was in the news for all the wrong reasons.

What was it about Luton? When I had been growing up there, the town had been something of a national joke, but recently it had been inextricably linked with Islamic radicalism. Only a few years earlier, a young British Pakistani, also from Luton and also called Manzoor, had been caught fighting against the British in Afghanistan, and more recently there were regular police raids on suspected extremists in my hometown. When friends asked me whether Luton was as bad as the media portrayed, I would strongly defend its reputation. That was why I had been so pleased with *Luton Actually*. I could present a

Courtesy Sergio Dionisio/ AP Images

While Manzoor strongly defends the dignity of his hometown of Luton after the London bombings on 7 July 2005, he felt compelled to prove he was not a 'bad Muslim.'

more positive depiction of Luton, and yet now the worst terrorist atrocity on British soil had been committed by four British Muslims who had chosen Luton to begin their journey to mass murder.

I returned home on the first weekend after the bombing. It was a tense time. Police were patrolling the Underground, and stopping and searching anyone whom they thought looked suspicious. As I boarded the train at King's Cross, I made sure I left my hold-all unzipped so that anyone suspecting me could see that I only had some clothes, my iPod and my copy of the New Yorker inside. I felt I had to prove that I was not a 'bad Muslim'.

When I arrived at Luton train station I jumped into a taxi to take me to my mother's home. I asked the taxi driver how things were in Luton following the bombings. 'See, me personally, I don't think they did it,' the taxi driver said.

'What, you mean, you don't think it was those four Muslims?' I asked.

'No way, I reckon it was the Jews who did it to make us Muslims look bad. Same as 9/11.'

I would hear such claims on a depressingly regular basis. Sometimes I would try arguing back, but eventually it was easier to try to circumvent the conversation altogether. For my brother, the negative publicity around Luton was damaging for his property business. 'Do you want to know who's to blame? Those bloody Arabs and North Africans,' he told me as we sat in his living room. 'Algerians and Moroccans and all that lot. They've got war in their blood and they come into our communities and start spreading it around. Most Pakistanis just want to be left alone to live their lives.'

It was true that the Pakistanis I knew in Luton, the ones who came to our home to drink tea and gossip with my mother, couldn't care less about international politics or foreign policy. But there were others, the ones who lurked outside the central mosque handing out leaflets, who did not feel the same. These were the Muslims who grabbed the headlines with their anger and hatred. They were the Muslims who were the most visible.

Why were they so angry and why did they hate this country so much? As someone who was also from Luton and who shared the same religion and nationality as these alienated and angry men, it sometimes felt in the days and weeks after 7/7 as if I was expected to speak for the bombers and in some way explain why they had bombed the tube. But in fact, when I heard those young British Muslims speak so contemptuously about living in this country, my reaction was one of anger, confusion and betrayal. What they felt and what they preached was not in my name.[1]

CONNECTIONS

1. Create an identity chart to capture the impact of the 7 July 2005 on Manzoor's identity. What words would you use to describe how he felt? What events shaped his response?

2. Manzoor writes that he did not want to be seen as a 'bad Muslim.' What does that mean to him? How does he hope to show others that he is not a bad Muslim? What does he hope the objects in his bag will reveal about his identity?

3. How do you want others to see you? What do you do to project that identity to others?

4. When Manzoor arrived in Luton, a Muslim taxi driver told him that the Jews were to blame for the attacks. Manzoor's brother thought that the perpatrators must be Arabs and North African Muslims rather than Pakistani Muslims. Why might they have blamed others?

5. Since 11 September 2001, conspiracy theorists have spread a false rumour that Jews were responsible for the terrorist attacks in New York and Washington. The rumors resurfaced after 7/7 despite the evidence and testimony by the perpetrators themselves. Why would these rumours take root? Scholars suggest that rumours, even false rumours, serve a purpose for the people who spread them. What purpose do these antisemitic rumours serve? For whom?

6. After the London attacks, many commentators suggested that the fact that the perpetrators of the attacks were British said a lot about the failure of integration? Do you agree?

7. Manzoor felt that he was asked to 'speak for the bombers and… explain why they had bombed the tube.' Why did people expect that Manzoor could speak for the bombers or explain their actions?

8. Manzoor makes it clear that the attacks were 'not in my name.' Some, however, have suggested that Muslims have an obligation to disavow terrorism and to apologize. Do you agree? At what point does expression of legitimate concerns become stereotyping of an entire group?

---

[1] Sarfraz Manzoor, *Greetings from Bury Park: A Memoir* (New York: Vintage Books, 2007), 261–64.

SLEEPWALKING TOWARDS SEGREGATION

Courtesy Cate Gillon/ Getty Images

With its abundant diversity Britain still has evidence of being segregated. Phillips' speech reminded his audience that it takes a conscious effort to establish integration.

In September 2005, just two months after the 7/7 terrorist attacks, Trevor Phillips, Chair of the Commission for Racial Equality, spoke to a crowd in Manchester, warning that Britain was 'sleepwalking towards segregation.'

> Integration is a learned competence—like maths or driving a car. It is not instinctive. And these skills determine whether events escalate or dampen down. In the way that they know what to say and what not to say, when to be firm, when to turn a blind eye ... These are very subtle skills, and where they are abundant, societies can cope with great shocks...
>
> In fact, I believe that time is becoming our enemy in the fight for an integrated society. ...We who live in London can all too often persuade ourselves, as we sit around the dinner table,

that we are a model for the world, because we eat exotic foods, we watch foreign films, we take our children to the park to play with children whose names are not like ours; and because we ourselves would never dream of discriminating racially.

But the writer Max Hastings, formerly the editor of both the Telegraph and the Evening Standard, where he made strenuous efforts to diversify his newsroom, cut through this smugness recently when he wrote that, having thought about it, he could not remember ever having invited a Muslim to his house, and rarely saw a black face at parties. I know he is right about the latter, since I was often one of those isolated black faces....

The fact is that we are a society which, almost without noticing it, is becoming more divided by race and religion. We are becoming more unequal by ethnicity. Our schools—and I mean the ordinary schools, not faith schools—are becoming more exclusive.

Our universities have started to become colour-coded, with virtual 'whites keep-out' signs in some urban institutions; and if you look closely at the campuses of some of our most distinguished universities, you can pick out the invisible 'no blacks need apply' messages.

Residentially, some districts are on their way to becoming fully fledged ghettoes—black holes into which no one goes without fear and trepidation, and from which no one ever escapes undamaged....

If we allow this to continue, we could end up in 2048, a hundred years on from the Windrush, living in a [segregated] Britain [with] passively co-existing ethnic and religious communities, eyeing each other uneasily over the fences of our differences.

...[T]he aftermath of 7/7 forces us to assess where we are. And here is where I think we are: we are sleepwalking our way to segregation. We are becoming strangers to each other, and we are leaving communities to be marooned outside the mainstream.[1]

CONNECTIONS ◈ ◈ ◈ ◈ ◈ ◈ ◈ ◈ ◈

1. Philips believes, 'Integration is a learned competence…. It is not instinctive.' What does he mean? Do you agree? If integration is a learned competence, how do you learn it?

2. If you were to measure social integration in your own community, where would you look? What would you look for?

3. Phillips describes a newspaper editor who worked hard to diversify his newsroom but 'could not remember ever inviting a Muslim to his house.' How do you explain why social segregation is often even stronger than segregation at school or in the workplace?

4. Phillips writes that he was often 'one of those isolated black faces.' Have you ever been the 'only one' in a group? What did it feel like?

5. Phillips warned his audiences that, 'we are sleepingwalking our way to segregation.' If Great Britain were to become more segregated, what would be the consequences?

[1] Trevor Phillips, 'After 7/7: Sleepwalking to Segregation', (speech, 22 September, 2005, Manchester, England) http://www.humanities.manchester.ac.uk/socialchange/research/social-change/summer-workshops/documents/sleepwalking.pdf (accessed 15 April 2009).

NEGOTIATING DIFFERENCES

Poet James Berry raises important questions about the way we respond to differences in the poem 'What Do You Do With a Variation?'

> What do we do with a difference?
> Do we stand and discuss its oddity
> or do we ignore it?
>
> Do we shut our eyes to it
> or poke it with a stick?
> Do we clobber it to death?
>
> Do we move around it in rage
> and enlist the rage of others?
> Do we will it to go away?
>
> Do we look at it in awe
> or purely in wonderment?
> Do we work for it to disappear?
>
> Do we pass it stealthily
> Or change route away from it?
> Do we will it to become like ourselves?
>
> What do we do with a difference?
> Do we communicate to it,
> let application acknowledge it
> for barriers to fall down?[1]

In England, and in Europe as a whole, much of the discussion of differences has focused on an increasingly visible Muslim population. Islam, to which many immigrants subscribe, has become a lightning rod for the role of religion in public life. These issues have only been heightened in the aftermath of the terrorist bombings in New York, Washington, Madrid, and London.

While Great Britain has an established religion, most people hardly notice the influence of the Church of England in British life. Perhaps no symbol has aroused as much conversation as Muslim head coverings. Jack Straw, the former Home Secretary, found himself in the middle of controversy when, after meeting with a Muslim constituent wearing a niqab (or a what he called the 'full veil'), he suggested that veils made integration difficult. In a weekly newspaper column, he explained his beliefs:

> It was not the first time I had conducted an interview with someone in a full veil, but this particular encounter, though very polite and respectful on both sides, got me thinking.
>
> In part, this was because of the apparent incongruity between the signals which indicate common bonds—the entirely English accent, the couples' education (wholly in the UK)—and the fact of the veil.
>
> Above all, it was because I felt uncomfortable about talking to someone 'face-to-face' who[m] I could not see.
>
> So I decided that I wouldn't just sit there the next time a lady turned up to see me in a full veil, and I haven't.
>
> Now, I always ensure that a female member of my staff is with me. I explain that this is a country built on freedoms. I defend absolutely the right of any woman to wear a headscarf. As for the full veil, wearing it breaks no laws.
>
> I go on to say that I think, however, that the conversation would be of greater value if the lady took the covering from her face.
>
> Indeed, the value of a meeting, as opposed to a letter or phone call, is so that you can—almost literally—see what the other person means, and not just hear what they say.
>
> However, I can't recall a single occasion when a lady has refused to lift her veil; most seem relieved I have asked.[2]

Straw asked another constituent:

> Would she, however, think hard about what I said—in particular about my concern that wearing the full veil was bound to make better, positive relations between the two communities more difficult.
>
> It was such a visible statement of separation and of difference.[3]

A Muslim woman wearing a niqab talks on a cell phone in East London.

Later Straw was interviewed on the BBC about the controversy. He explained:

> This is an issue that needs to be discussed because, in our society, we are able to relate particularly to strangers by being able to read their faces and if you can't read people's faces, that does provide some separation.
>
> Now I understand, of course, why some of these ladies decide to wear the veil.
>
> … I had a really good discussion with a lady last Friday—it was not because, contrary to myth, that she'd been required to do so by her husband—she'd come to her own decision about this.
>
> She said she felt more comfortable when she was outside wearing the veil and she was less troubled by people. I understand that.
>
> What I'm saying on the other side is: would those people who do wear the veil think about the implications for community relations?

He continued to explain his thinking on BBC Radio 4:

> What I've been struck (by) when I've been talking to some of the ladies concerned is that they had not, I think, been fully aware of the potential in terms of community relations.
>
> They'd thought of it just as a statement for themselves; in some cases they regard themselves as very religious—and I respect that, but as I say, I just wanted to put this issue on the table.
>
> Communities are bound together partly by informal chance relations between strangers, people acknowledging each other in the street, being able to pass the time of day, sharing just experiences in the street, and that is just made more difficult if people are wearing a veil…that's just a fact of life….
>
> I come to this out of a profound commitment to equal rights for Muslim communities and an equal concern about adverse development about parallel communities.[4]

Carla Power provides a different perspective on Jack Straw's interaction with the fully veiled woman:

> When British member of Parliament Jack Straw complained that it was hard to interact properly with the women who came to his office wearing niqabs, many Britons agreed. The democratic process was undermined, suggested the British press, by the women who were effectively faceless. Few noticed that they were there to see their Member of Parliament, exercising their rights as taxpaying citizens to engage in dialogue with their elected representative, something their migrant mothers and grandmothers probably never would have known to do, or dared.[5]

CONNECTIONS ◆ ◆ ◆ ◆ ◆ ◆ ◆ ◆ ◆

1. How have you learned what differences between people matter? What kinds of differences do you notice? Class? Skin colour? Gender? Accents? Religion? Are there any differences that make you uncomfortable? How do you respond to those differences?

2. How does the poem 'What Do You Do With a Variation?' connect to Jack Straw's story? Why did the 'full veil' matter to him?

3. Why do you think some differences matter more than others? What factors influence the way people respond to differences?

4. According to Straw, what makes integration possible? What gets in the way?

5. To what extent should the burden of integration fall on newcomers? What kinds of accommodations should members of the dominant society be willing to make?

6. Do you agree with Straw's perspective? What arguments does he use to support his suggestions? If you do not agree with Straw, what arguments might you use? How would you try to convince him to support your position?

---

[1] James Berry, 'What Do We Do With a Variation?' *When I Dance* (Orlando: Harcourt Brace, 1991).

[2] 'In Quotes: Jack Straw on the Veil', *BBC News*, 6 October, 2006, http://news.bbc.co.uk/2/hi/uk_news/polotics/5413470.stm (accessed 15 April 2009).

[3] Ibid.

[4] Ibid.

[5] Carla Power, 'Muslim Integration', (working paper, 10 September 2008).

CHANGING COMMUNITIES

Religious diversity is changing old assumptions about the proper relationship between church and state. In Great Britain, these questions are particularly complicated because the nation has an officially established Church: The Church of England.

An editorial from *The Economist* explains:

> England has an established church whose authority has been intertwined with the state's for five centuries. The powers of the Church of England have been trimmed and privileges have been granted to other religions. Yet although a mere 1.7 m[illion] people attend its services regularly, its special status endures. The queen is its head; Parliament approves its prayer book; and only last year [2007] did the prime minister relinquish the right to select its bishops, 25 of whom sit in the House of Lords.[1]

Courtesy Hazel Thompson/The New York Times/ Redux

Sheraz Arshad stands at the former Mount Zion Methodist Church, which will become a mosque. Mr. Arshad fought for years to get Clitheroe to allow a place for Muslims to worship.

In a particularly visible sign of Great Britain's new diversity, the former Mount Zion Methodist Church in Clitheroe has recently become a Mosque. *New York Times* writer Hazel Thompson tells the story:

> On a chilly night this winter, this pristine town in some of Britain's most untouched countryside voted to allow a former Christian church to become a mosque.
>
> The narrow vote by the municipal authorities marked the end of a bitter struggle by the tiny Muslim population to establish a place of worship, one that will put a mosque in an imposing stone Methodist church that had been used as a factory since its congregation dwindled away 40 years ago.
>
> The battle underscored Britain's unease with its Muslim minority…whose devotion has challenged an increasingly secular Britain's sense of itself.
>
> Britain may continue to regard itself as a Christian nation. But practising Muslims are likely to outnumber church-attending Christians in several decades, according to a recent survey by Christian Research, a group that specializes in documenting the status of Christianity in Britain.
>
> …In Clitheroe, the tussle involved a passionate young professional of Pakistani descent coming up against the raw nerves of tradition-bound local residents.
>
> 'We've been trying to get a place of worship for 30 years,' said Sheraz Arshad, 31, the Muslim leader here, his voice rattling around the empty old Mount Zion Methodist Church that will house his mosque. 'It's fitting it is a church: it is visually symbolic, the coming together of religions.'
>
> With a population of 14,500, a Norman castle and an Anglican church established in 1122, Clitheroe is tucked away in Lancashire County in the north. People here liked to think they represented a last barrier to the mosques that had become features in surrounding industrial towns. But Clitheroe had not bargained on the determination of Mr Arshad, a project manager at British Aerospace. He is the British-born son of Mohamed Arshad, who came to Clitheroe from Rawalpindi

[in Pakistan] in 1965 to work at the cement works on the town's outskirts.

When his father died in 2000, leaving his efforts to establish a mosque for the approximately 300 Muslims unfulfilled, Mr Arshad took up the challenge.

'I thought, why should I be treated any less well?' Mr Arshad said. 'One quarter of my salary goes in tax, too. I was driven to do the mosque.'

In all, Mr Arshad and his father made eight applications for a mosque....

Often there was booing at council meetings, and, he said, cries of 'Go home, Paki!'

The authorities' official reasoning for the rejections was generally that a mosque would attract outsiders—a veiled reference to Muslims—to Clitheroe.

...Mr Arshad decided to get organized and demonstrate that he was a moderate Muslim who could take part in all the town's affairs.

He formed an interfaith scout group—Beaver Scouts—that honoured many religious occasions, including the Taoist and Jewish New Years. He established the Medina Islamic Education Centre as an interfaith group for adults, and persuaded the local council to allow the group to lead a key committee. He organized a series of lectures on global conflict that attracted important academics.

On Dec. 21, the night of the vote on the mosque, the council chambers overflowed with 150 people. The police were poised outside. The vote was 7 to 5 for the mosque; there was no violence.

'I went in resigned to the fact we would lose,' Mr Arshad said. 'In the end, it was very humbling.'

'The church's [listing] as a place of worship in the town's planning records helped carry the day,' said Geoffrey Jackson, chief executive of Trinity Partnership, a social welfare agency, and a Methodist who backed Mr Arshad.

So did Mr Arshad's demeanour. 'He's a top lad, with a Lancashire accent, born and bred here, and educated at Clitheroe Grammar,' Mr Jackson said.[2]

CONNECTIONS ◆ ◆ ◆ ◆ ◆ ◆ ◆ ◆ ◆

1. What is the role of religious institutions in the life of a community? Why do you think religion plays an important role in immigrant communities? How do those answers explain why it was important for Arshad to build a local mosque?

2. Islamic scholar Riem Spielhaus explains, 'Each [mosque building] conflict presents an opportunity to open communication because they raise rarely discussed issues.' What issues do those conflicts raise? How can these conflicts be turned into opportunities to promote integration?

3. How do you explain the initial resistance to Arshad's proposal at the town council meetings? What role did fear play? How did Arshad overcome that resistance?

---

[1] 'Sever them', *The Economist*, 14 February 2008, http://www.economist.com/opinion/displaystory.cfm?story id=10689643 (accessed 17 March 2008).
[2] Jane Perlez, 'Old Church Becomes Mosque in Uneasy Britain', *The New York Times*, 2 April 2007, http://www.nytimes.com/2007/04/02/world/europe/02britian.html?pagewanted=print (accessed 8 November 2009).

Three Parables of Integration

Nations, similar to individuals, have identities. Some people believe those identities are derived from a shared language, ethnicity, or even pseudo-scientific ideas about 'race.' Others point to common historical experiences. Sociologist Benedict Anderson believes differently. He explains that nations are 'imagined communities' that do not exist in blood, territory, or history. Instead they are:

> …an imagined political community. …It is imagined because the members of even the smallest nation will never know most of their fellow-members, meet them, or even hear of them, yet in the minds of each lives the image of their communion.[1]

The Chief Rabbi of the British Commonwealth, Sir Jonathan Sacks, uses three different parables about integrating newcomers to a nation. This reading contains excerpts from Sacks', *The Home We Build Together*:

> In the first, a hundred strangers have been wandering around the countryside in search of a place to stay. Eventually they arrive at the gate of a large country house. The owner comes to the gate, sees the strangers and asks them who they are. They tell him their story. He gives them a warm smile. 'How good to see you,' he says. 'As you can see, I have an enormous home. Far too big for me, actually. There are hundreds of empty rooms. Please feel free to stay here as long as you like. I look forward to your company. From now on consider yourselves my guests.'
>
> A lovely story. But not entirely so for the strangers in the long run. They have a place to live, and yes, their host is exactly as he seemed at first, welcoming, hospitable. … However there is only one thing wrong as far as they are concerned. However generous their host, he remains the host and they are his guests. The place belongs to someone else. That is society as a country house.

The second: A hundred strangers in search of a home find themselves in the middle of a big city. They are there to find a hotel. It is large, comfortable, and has every amenity. The visitors have money enough to pay the hotel bills. They book their rooms, unpack, and stay. The rules are simple. They are free to do what they like, so long as they don't disturb the other guests. Their relationship with the hotel is purely contractual. They pay money in return for certain services. . . .

The hotel offers the newcomers a freedom and equality they did not have in the first model. They are guests, but so is everyone else. There is only one problem. A hotel is where you stay, not where you belong. You feel no loyalty to a hotel. You don't put down roots there. It doesn't become part of your identity. . . .Yes, after a while you recognize your fellow guests. You bid them good morning. You discuss the weather and football. But it remains a place where everyone is, in the biblical phrase, 'a stranger and sojourner.' That is society as a hotel.

The third: A hundred strangers arrive at a town. They are met by the mayor, councillors and local residents. The mayor says: 'Friends, we welcome you. It is good to have you among us. Sadly, as you can see, there is no country house where we might accommodate you. There is, though, something we can offer you.

'We have a patch of empty land: large enough to accommodate homes for all of you. We have bricks and materials. We have experts who can help you design your homes, and we will help you build them. . . .Let us do this together.'

So it happens. Unlike the country house, the newcomers have to build their own long-term accommodation. Unlike the hotel, they do not merely pay. They invest their energies in what they build. . . They helped build it.

The diversity of Britain has become increasingly visible.

Sacks explains that it won't always be easy.

> The newcomers still occasionally seem strange. They speak
> and act and dress differently from the locals. But those long
> sessions of working together have had their effect. The locals
> know the newcomers are serious, committed, dedicated. They
> have their own ways, but they have also learned the ways of
> the people of the town, and they have worked out . . . a rough
> and ready friendship. . . . Making something together breaks
> down walls of suspicion and misunderstanding. . . . That is
> society as the home we build together.[2]

CONNECTIONS

1. How do newcomers learn to adapt to their new nation? How do communities learn to accommodate what Sacks calls strangers'?

2. Sacks offers three parables—stories with a moral—as metaphors for types of integration. What lesson is he trying to teach with each of these stories?

3. When is someone no longer a 'stranger'?

4. What does it mean to be assimilated? What does it mean to be integrated? What is the difference?

[1] Benedict Anderson, *Imagined Communities: Reflections on the Origin and Spread of Nationalism* (London and New York, Verson) 1991, 577.
[2] Jonathan Sacks, *The Home We Build Together* (New York: Continuum, 2008) 15-15.

CREDITS

Immigration and Identity: 'Search For My Tongue,' from *Brunizem* by Sujata Bhatt. Copyright © 1988. Reprinted with permission from Carcanet Press Limited.

An Island of Immigrants: 'Migration From a Second Generation Perspective,' by Amanda Huxtable from Moving Here: 200 Years of Migration to England. Copyright © Amanda Huxtable. Reprinted with permission.

The Cricket Test: From 'Rethinking Cricket Test Loyalty,' by Mangala Nanda. Reprinted with permission. 'Am I Doubted Because I'm a Jew?' © Telegraph Media Group Limited 2009. Reprinted with permission.

Religion and Belonging: Excerpts from 'We've Ditched Race for Religion,' by Sarfaz Manzoor as published in the *The Guardian* on January 11, 2005. Reprinted with permission. www.sarfazmanzoor.co.uk. From 'Revenge of young Muslims,' by Yasmin Hai. Copyright © *The Sunday Times*, April 6, 2008. Reprinted with permission.

Teaching Britishness: From '24th May-Empire Day for Queen and the Country!' Historic UK website, http://www.historic-uk.com/HistoryUK/England-History/EmpireDay.htm (accessed April 14, 2009). Reprinted with permission.

Accommodating Differences: From 'Multiculturalism Starts Losing Its Luster,' by Theodore Dalrymple. © City Journal (Summer 2004). Reprinted with permission.

Turning Points: Copyright Guardian News & Media Ltd 2007. 'The Day I Realised Music Could Change the World,' by Billy Bragg. Reprinted with permission. Copyright Guardian News & Media Ltd 2006. 'The Struggle For Belonging,' by Billy Bragg. Reprinted with permission.

Fitting In: Copyright Guardian News & Media Ltd 2007. 'Under My Skin,' by Shane Meadows. Reprinted with permission.